BUSINESS RESOURCES FOR INSPIRING LEADERS

GET IT DONE!

Design the Business of Your Dreams

Table of Contents

GET IT DONE! Design the Business of Your Dreams

Does starting your own business make you feel like you are diving into the deep end of a swimming pool while it is still being filled up with water? You're not alone. Likely you are excited and terrified at the same time. Maybe you can't wait to get your feet wet with your own business and yet you may be so busy treading water – taking actions without results - that it can feel hard to stay afloat. Or worse, you are drowning in too much information without the right direction.

Do any of these statements sound like you?

- Have a side hustle that you would like to turn into a full-time business;
- Have been thinking of starting your own business;
- Want to be your own boss but you have no idea where to start;
- Want to learn from amazing, relatable, and successful business women.

Don't worry! We see you with your arms waving in the air, looking for help! You have found the right book with advice for starting your business.
But what if you currently have your own business? Are you struggling with the following issues?

- Your business is growing but your path to success feels scary and uncertain;
- Your business is not growing at the rate you want;

- You've been struggling to figure out how to put systems in place to get the most − and give the most − to your business;
- You don't know how to take your business to the next level.

We're here for you, too! You have found the right book with tricks, tips and tested secrets for building your business to fit your vision of success.

Being successful as an entrepreneur requires motivation, dedication, and a vision. It also means being skilled in many different areas. You have a product or service to sell so you need to understand sales. Yet you also have clients relying on you so you need to know customer service. And of course, you have finances related to your business so you need to understand accounting. And there are many more required skills. But how do you as one person know how to tackle all of these proficiently?

If all these thoughts are running through your mind, or you wake up in the middle of the night worrying about your business, we want to tell you that you are not alone. We are here to offer knowledge, help and support. All the women who have contributed to this book are not just experts in their field, but also successful business owners in their own right, with over 150 years of experience among them in their fields of expertise, most of those years spent as entrepreneurs.

It can take years to master many business skills. However, we're here to share that there are shortcuts you can adopt. The ideas shared in this book will make your journey to success easier and shorter. Listening to other successful female entrepreneurs will help you avoid some of the pitfalls they faced and find a quicker road to success.

If you're diving into the metaphorical entrepreneurial swimming pool – or you are in the deep end and looking for relief – and you need help, you call the lifeguard, right? Similarly, if you're starting your own business and you need assistance, you can read the amazing advice in this book and call on the expertise of these ten authors. Think of them as your entrepreneurial lifeguards.

For you, we have compiled amazing advice from ten enterprising entrepreneurial women who are at the top in their fields. Together, these lady bosses have hundreds of years of experience with:

- What it takes to be a leader in today's economy;
- Structuring your business to be successful;
- Networking and connecting with the people who will help you succeed;
- Utilizing social media and the hottest content to attract your ideal clients;
- Understanding the personalities of your clients to land more and larger sales;
- Improving your retention rate for your existing awesome clients;
- Knowing the correct information to keep your business out of tax trouble;
- Ensuring you are preparing for a bright financial future when you retire;
- Getting the most from current trends to keep your business fresh.

Get ready to dive in with our ten experts who can help you swim to success!

4

Why Leaders Need Emotional Intelligence

Diana Parra

Today's leaders need emotional intelligence or EI to greatly and positively influence those around them. Whether you are leading a company, a team, a church, your students, or your family and children, the need is still the same. Research has shown time and time again that leaders with a high degree of EI are more effective.

Let me share with you why EI is important to me. For about ten years, I struggled with unresolved emotions stemming from a series of challenging life events; relocating across the country, the loss of my father to cancer, lack of a support system, four miscarriages, the adoption of three children, the challenges that came with the adoption, a brief period of separation from my husband, the start of a business, and stress. Lots and lots of stress. This all culminated in health challenges and more stress. Now keep in mind that I have a background in psychology and worked as a therapist for many years. You would think that I should have handled these experiences much better. However, although I have the degrees and lots of experience with helping others, I was no good at helping myself. Why? I later found out that level of education and a high IQ are not the best predictors of personal and professional success. In fact, the best predictor of success and fulfillment in your personal and professional life is your EI.

EI is the foundation for critical skills and impacts what you say and do daily. It is the strongest driver of leadership and personal excellence and is also linked to the ability to make more money.

There are two important words that I want you to keep in mind: Leader and Performance. A leader is anyone with a sphere of influence - YOU. Performance does not simply depend on technical expertise; it relies on our ability to understand and relate to others and ourselves.

What is EI?

The term "Emotional Intelligence" or EI was coined by Peter Salovey and John D. Mayer in 1990. It is used to describe "a form of social intelligence that involves the ability to monitor one's own and others' feelings and emotions, to discriminate among them, and to use this information to guide one's thinking and action."

Basically, EI is the ability to recognize emotions in yourself and others, and the ability to use this awareness to manage your behavior and relationships.

This ability gives individuals a variety of skills. They are better able to manage relationships, navigate social networks, and influence and inspire others. Each of us possess our own level of EI, but to become effective leaders, we need a high level of emotional intelligence. In today's world, EI has become an important factor for success, efficiency, productivity, and collaboration.

The Four Skills of EI

EI is composed of four skills. The first two are about you - Personal Competence. The other two are about how you interact with others - Social Competence.

Personal Competence Skills

Self-Awareness
People with EI have the ability to recognize their own emotions and how they affect their thoughts, behaviors, and their effect on others. For example, a leader who flies off the handle because they don't recognize they are under stress and is therefore, impatient, will focus on what others do wrong. This leader will have a negative impact on morale and motivation regardless of whether they are leading a company, team, family, etc. The result will be the same. People will dislike having any interaction with that person and may even avoid them. This conduct does not promote trust or collaboration. Most of us don't realize how this behavior is counterproductive. If we don't develop self-awareness, the issue is difficult to recognize. Most people want and respect a leader who can stay calm and collected when facing challenging situations. Leaders with a high EI know the consequences of their reactions and behaviors and are aware of the impact these have on others.

Self-Management
Leaders with high EI can self-regulate and stay in control. This means they can control impulsive feelings and behaviors. They are thoughtful about their actions and can easily adapt to changing circumstances. They are unlikely to let their anger take control or to make hasty decisions. This makes them highly respected by others.

Social Competence Skills

Social Awareness
People with this ability can pick up on emotional cues in other people and understand them. Being able to perceive what others are thinking and feeling even when you don't feel the same way

is a sign of high EI. A leader who has high social competence will be comfortable socially. Listening and observing are paramount. This means we must stop talking, stop thinking ahead about what we are going to say next, stop anticipating what the other person is going to say, and simply listen to the other person.

Relationship Management
Leaders who use relationship management to become aware of their own emotions and those of others manage interactions successfully. These leaders are highly skilled at developing and maintaining good relationships.

Why EI Makes Leaders More Effective

EI can be a key differentiator when it comes to leadership. Leaders who score high on EI communicate clearly, and inspire and influence others. These are the leaders who are true catalysts for change and make a greater impact.

The following are some areas/skills in which leadership performance is improved through EI:

Effective Communication
EI makes leaders more self-aware, which in turn allows them to have insight and a better understanding of other people's strengths and weaknesses. This allows everyone to be on the same page, understanding what is expected or needed from them. Part of effective communication is effective listening. This means listening without judgement, keeping emotions under control, and asking questions when necessary to seek to understand.

Empathy
This is the ability to "put yourself in someone else's shoes." This is a key component of successful human relationships. Empathy helps a leader understand the circumstances others are facing, and how those circumstances impact their work and performance. Asking yourself why someone does what they do will lead to a more productive conversation than if you focus on the "problematic" behavior. Empathy is critical to managing a successful team or organization.

Conflict Resolution
Leaders with a high EI are highly skilled at handling conflict and providing resolution. This means a better work and home environment. Resolving conflict in a healthy, constructive way can strengthen trust between people. When conflict isn't perceived as threatening, it can foster creativity and trust in relationships and can in fact strengthen them.

Improves Physical Health
Managing your emotions makes you better at managing your stress. We are all aware of the negative effects that stress has on our physical well-being, including higher risk of heart attack, high blood pressure, and suppressed immune system, to name a few.

Improves Mental Health
Uncontrolled emotions and stress can negatively impact your mental health. If you are unable to understand and manage your emotions, you can be at risk for anxiety and depression. As a result, the ability to build strong, close relationships can be a struggle. This can lead to feelings of isolation and loneliness.

How Can You Increase Your EI?

Here are a few strategies you can put into practice to increase and strengthen your emotional intelligence.

Self-Awareness
Move towards your emotions, especially the ones that cause discomfort such as anger, fear, and confusion. Ask yourself why you feel that way. Explore this. It will highlight where you need to do the work/change.

Self-Management
Often, we can't see it ourselves. Talking to a third party about a problem can bring clarity and understanding. Someone who is not emotionally invested in your problem can give you a fresh and unbiased perspective to improve your self-management.

Social Awareness
Listen, listen, listen. Stop doing everything else while the other person is talking. Make eye contact, sit close to them if possible, and put your cell phone and laptop away. Focus on what they are saying, notice their expressions and body language, and ask for clarification. Fully engage with the person. Be fully present.

Relationship Management
Trust an integral part of relationships. For there to be trust between people, they need to know each other at some level. Share something about yourself with the other person. Be consistent in your words, actions, and behavior, and make sure you follow through on commitments. Be open in your communication to avoid misunderstandings. And ask the other person what needs to happen to build trust.

If we want to experience personal and professional success, we must first develop robust EI skills. We need to first assess where we are and then determine where the work needs to be done. Increasing our EI will strengthen our self-awareness and our capacity to understand others leading to stronger and healthier relationships; beginning with the most important one- the one with ourselves.

Diana Parra, M.A.
Founder and CEO
Akros Leadership International, LLC

Diana Parra, M.A. is a leadership and transformational strategist and a high-performance coach for executives. She is the founder and CEO of Akros Leadership International. Her passion is teaching female entrepreneurs and small business owners how to lead themselves first so they can lead others successfully and have a greater impact on the world. She founded Akros to create a community of leaders dedicated to empowering and inspiring others by leading with love and compassion, while elevating the world at large. Her 20 plus years of combined experience as a manager, therapist, coach, and consultant have forged in her a unique approach to leadership development. She holds a Bachelor's degree in Psychology from Rutgers University and a Master's degree in Educational Psychology with a concentration in Clinical Psychology from Montclair State University.

She was born in Colombia, is bilingual and bi-cultural, and is married to her best friend. She has three adoptive children, is an explorer of the world, a lover of self-development, music, yoga, and nature.

Phone: 804.286.2426

Website: www.akrosinternational.com

Structuring Your Business for Success
Stinson Mundy

Congratulations! Starting a business can be one of the most exciting (and terrifying) adventures you'll ever take. Google "how to start a business" and you'll be hit with information overload – articles telling you everything from what steps to take to what not to do. And while setting up the actual legal structure of your business can be simple, there is much more that should go into it than just filing your paperwork and grabbing an Employee Identification Number (EIN.) Taking time on the front end to think through what you hope your business will become, how it will grow, and what your exit plans looks like can help ensure that the business you establish today helps you meet those goals. Before you start working with your first client or sell your first product, here are the four things that every business should do to structure itself for success.

Assemble Your External Advisory Team

You know what you want to sell, and you may even have an idea of how you will sell it. Better yet, you're an expert in your field (or soon to be one.) As you get ready to launch your idea into the world, now is the time to assemble your external advisory team to help guide you through the areas of business ownership that are foreign to you. Your external advisory team should include the following:

Accountant / Bookkeeper
An accountant is an individual or company that helps you and your business with your finances and prepares your taxes.

Sometimes your accountant will also help set up and maintain your books. Your accountant can help you determine any taxes the business will be responsible for paying (i.e. sales tax, business taxes, etc.) and answer any tax related questions you will have.

Business Attorney
A business attorney is an attorney who focuses their practice on business law and can help you determine your corporate structure, set up your owner agreements, prepare the agreements you have with your clients, and provide guidance for other areas you may need assistance (i.e. intellectual property, real estate, etc.).

Banker
Your banker is an individual who works for the bank where you keep your business accounts. Your banker will help you establish the best accounts for your business and help you access other types of capital (i.e. line of credit, SBA loan, etc.)

Marketer
A marketer is an individual or company that helps you identify who your target audience is and then develops a strategy to help you reach that audience. Your marketer may also help you execute that strategy (i.e. sponsorships, advertising, etc.)

Each of these individuals is a subject matter expert. By leveraging their expertise, you can ensure that your business has a strong foundation from which to launch.

Choose the Legal Structure that Fits Best with Your Business

There are four main ways that a business can choose to be structured:

1. Sole Proprietorship

2. Partnership

3. Corporation

4. Limited Liability Company.

While the terms get used interchangeably, they each are very distinct legal entities. Before you can file the paperwork to establish yourself as a company, you need to determine which form your business will take.

Sole Proprietor
This is the most basic business form when you, as an individual, sell your goods or services without any formal legal structure. Any money you earn goes directly into your bank account (although you could have a separate one if you chose) and your income (and expenses) are accounted for on your personal income taxes. While Sole Proprietorships are very simple to get started, one of the biggest downsides is that you (and your personal assets) are responsible for any of your businesses debts and liabilities. Most side hustles (and many other businesses) get started this way because it can be as easy as grabbing a business license and selling your products.

Partnership

When two or more individuals come together to conduct business together, they form a partnership. Within the partnership, they pool their resources and share in the income and expenses. Generally, each partner is liable for the businesses debts and liabilities, which can put the individual's assets as risk. Like a sole proprietorship, partners account for income (and expenses) on their personal income taxes. Partnerships are often seen with professional services (accounting firms, law firms, architects), where the individuals exchange time for money but could benefit from shared resources, like an office, administrative staff, etc.

Corporation

Corporations are the most formal and traditional legal structure. The corporation is owned by one or more shareholders (who own stock) and is governed by a board of directors. When operated properly, the shareholders are not responsible for the corporation's debts or liabilities, which protects the shareholders personal assets. The corporation pays its own taxes and then shareholders are responsible for paying taxes on any individual dividends or distributions they receive.

Limited Liability Company

Today, the limited liability company ("LLC") is the entity du jour. LLCs combine the liability protections of a corporation with the taxing benefits of sole proprietorship / partnership. LLC's are easy to establish and don't require the corporate formalities that come with a Corporation.

Determining which entity works best for you and your business depends on a lot of factors. What is your business? Who owns it? What are your capitalization plans? What is your end game? And while an LLC structure can work for many businesses, it's not always the right choice. Talk through your business plans with your attorney and accountant to ensure that you're set up in way that helps you reach your goals.

Set Client Expectations

Regardless of the type of business you run, and whether you realize it or not, you enter into agreements with your clients. These agreements lay out your expectations for how the relationship will operate. Common types of client agreements include:

Service Agreements
These agreements spell out what services you will provide to your clients, your fees, how and when the services will be performed, and spell out the details of your relationship.

Terms of Use/Privacy Policies
These documents govern how your clients can access your website and what they can do with the information it contains. For example, if you provide content on your website, your Terms of Use policy details how someone can use the content after they download it, whether they can share it and what they can expect from you going forward.

Return Policies
If you sell a product, your return policy governs how and when you customer can return or exchange product, and whether they will receive a refund, a partial refund or store credit.
Take the time to determine how you want your client relationship to work. Envision your worst-case scenario and then make sure that your attorney drafts your agreements to protect you.

Take Steps to Protect Your Proprietary Information and Intellectual Property

Now that you have your idea, you've met with your advisory team, and you've started thinking about how you and your clients will interact, you need to think through how you will protect your proprietary information and your brand. These protections take many forms and some of the most common include:

Non-Disclosure Agreements
This agreement governs the sharing of confidential and proprietary information. The parties agree not to disclose any of the information shared with them during their relationship to third-parties and if they do, whether intentionally or inadvertently, the agreement spells out how each party can enforce their rights.

Trademark / Service Mark
A trademark is a word, phrase, symbol, or design that informs the public where the product comes from – i.e. your logo, your tagline, your business name. Trademarks are for physical goods and service marks are for services. There are state and federal trademark protections available.

Copyright
A copyright is the exclusive right of the creator of a piece of work (writings, photographs, film, etc.) to publish, sell, reproduce and distribute the work.

Patent
A patent is a legal right to make or sell an invention.

License Agreements

License agreements allow you to use a third-party's trademark, service mark, patent, or other product / service for a specified purpose and time-period. You might also license your intellectual property to other for use in their businesses.

Given all the time you'll spend bringing your business to life, it is essential that you take some time and make sure that its protected.

Spending time on these four areas – your external team, your corporate structure, your client relationships, and protecting your business – before you launch is one of the best investments you can make in your business. These lay the foundations for everything else you want to accomplish and can help you start your adventure on a solid footing.

~~~~~

This article is for informational purposes only and does not constitute legal advice nor does it create an attorney-client relationship. Always consult appropriate legal counsel for specific questions related to your business. Some states may consider this attorney advertising.

C. Stinson Mundy, Esq.
Linden Legal Strategies PLLC

C. Stinson Mundy, Esq. is the founder of Linden Legal Strategies PLLC, a Richmond, Virginia based law firm that focuses on business law and development. Stinson has spent her career helping companies solve business problems. After earning her degree at the University of Richmond School of Law, she started her career at one of Richmond's preeminent boutique law firms, helping businesses of all sizes. After that, she served as General Counsel for a national transportation company headquartered locally where she helped solve complicated business and legal problems every day. In 2016 she founded Linden Legal Strategies to remove the obstacles many businesses face when seeking legal services. Her distinctive approach and flat-rate pricing opens the door to big-picture thinking, deeper relationships and open communication with clients.

Phone: 804.215.0175

Email: stinson@lindenlegalstrategies.com

How My Story Led Me to Connect with Women on My Path

Shanna Kabatznick

Hi there! I'm Shanna, the founder of FABWOMEN, an organization I created to help women be Fearless, Authentic and Bold – or FAB! My goal is to continue growing and fostering a community where women can feel safe to connect, build relationships, learn and grow their business. But this crazy idea of mine didn't just happen out of thin air. My own journey and experiences shaped my vision for what you see today. I'd like to share my story with you to demonstrate the value of feeling connected.

I was born and raised in Quito, Ecuador, to an American Jewish father and beautiful Spanish Catholic mother. Quite the combination, right? Every summer, we would vacation in the United States with my grandparents. What I didn't realize was this time spent every year would eventually shape my life. I'll never forget this pivotal conversation with my father.

"Shanna?"

"Yes, Dad."

"Your mother and I, we love you very much. You know that, right?"

"Yes, Dad. Of course, I know that."

"Well, because we love you so much, we have decided that you're not going to continue this vacation with us. Instead, we have enrolled you in college here in the United States."

You can imagine the shock that went through my system after this conversation. My world was just rocked. I didn't feel ready for such a massive change. Seeing my trepidation, my Dad tried to reassure me.

"Don't worry. We met some really nice people and they will get you all squared away and set up."

Realizing it was a futile effort to try and argue with my Dad, I asked the next logical question.

"So, where am I going?"

"Starkville, Mississippi, Mississippi State University."

I'd never heard of this town. As a matter of fact, Starkville was so small, when my dad pulled out a map to show me, we couldn't even find it!

The next few days were a bit of a blur. Things were happening so fast, and I barely had enough time to process what was happening. I remember lots of shopping, and before I knew it, we were saying our tearful good-byes and I was off to Mississippi State. How did I get here?

My parents had literally adopted the 'sink or swim' mentality, and now that I was in a new country with a new culture, I knew I had better learn to swim. When I arrived at Mississippi State, I was fortunate to have a roommate that welcomed me with true southern hospitality. She took me under her wing and showed me the ropes. Let's just say, culture shock is real. I quickly learned how different things were in the U.S. compared to my home country of Ecuador. Let me share a few examples.

The first time I went out to eat in the States, I asked for a hamburger. Now, we eat hamburgers in Ecuador, too, but when you ask for a hamburger there, you get a hamburger, plain. That's normal. Here, in the States, it's quite different. If you ask for a hamburger, there are a million choices of toppings, from grilled onions, lettuce, tomato, ketchup, mustard, and I can go on. Fortunately, my English was pretty good because I grew up bi-lingual. But, I'd yet to master the southern Mississippi dialect which often took me by surprise. While I was acclimating to my unfamiliar environment, I just learned to say "yes" when asked what I wanted, just to make things simpler.

On another occasion, I noticed my dirty clothes pile growing, so I asked my roommate, "when is the cleaning lady coming?" She asked me to grab my clothes so we could find her. I got my clothes together and we walked downstairs to a room full of washers and driers. My roommate looks at me and says, "Here's some detergent and some quarters. You just met your cleaning lady." I stood there for a moment, a bit shell-shocked. I'd never washed my own clothes before, but I was about to learn quickly. It was trial by fire. The good news is, I did learn to do my own laundry, but not before turning a few things pink. Colors and whites don't mix in the laundry.

One of my funniest stories happened during the summer that I spent with my friends in Washington, D.C. I was excited about this experience because what better way to learn the American culture! We planned to spend July 4th at the Capitol. My friends kept telling me that we were going to the Mall on July 4th. I kept asking myself, "why are going shopping on July 4th and how are we going to watch the fireworks?" I eventually figured it all out.

After I graduated college, I followed the status quo. I found a good job, met someone, got married, bought a house, and had two kids. Happily, ever after, right? Wrong! One of my first life lessons was that things don't always go as planned, no matter how meticulous the plan is. I found myself alone again, but this time I was a single mother with two children. I asked myself the question once again, "how did I get here?"

How often do you ask yourself the same question? Let me tell you what was different about my scenario at this juncture in my life. I held the controls over what was next. Not my father. Not my husband. Me. And, it was empowering. I had the choice to grab my kids and go back home to Ecuador or I could choose to stand up and press forward into the great unknown. I don't know about you, but the second choice seemed more exciting. Was I afraid? Of course, but I did it anyway. The definition of courage isn't the absence of fear, it is pressing on through it, and that is exactly what I did.

As I learned to navigate through life alone once again, this time in Richmond, Virginia, I wondered how many other women experienced the same feeling. How many women need that feeling of connection, that empowerment and strength? That is how FABWOMEN was born. I wanted to create an environment to nurture women with all the things I was missing as I went through major transitions in my life. FABWOMEN is a community of women who come together, embrace life, their authenticity, and learn from each other both personally and professionally.

As I reflect on the scared 18-year-old girl from Ecuador experiencing life in the States for the first time to the woman I've become today – wow, what a journey! And, I'm still growing every day. Through this FABulous journey, I've learned the value and importance of connecting with others. Regardless of our background, we all need to be connected to others, and FABWOMEN celebrates that. The next time you are in a place wondering, "how did I get here?", remember that you have a choice. What will it be?

Shanna Kabatznick
Founder and CEO
FABWOMEN

My name is Shanna Kabatznick and I am the Founder and CEO of **FAB**WOMEN. The road to creating **FAB**WOMEN was not an easy one. It was paved with many detours all leading me to something I could have never imagined. I was born in Quito, Ecuador to a Spanish Catholic mom and an American Jewish dad. Needless to say, I learned to embraced diversity early on and as I have grown it has truly become something I continue to cherish and learn from.

After graduating high school, I came to the United States for College where I went to Mississippi State University. (Yes, I speak more on this topic at some of my presentations). The rest of my story is a fairly traditional one. I finished college, stayed in the States, got a job, settled down, had kids and lived happily ever after. Wait that is not exactly how it happened.

Detour #1 – I did not settle down! Due to my husband's work we moved a lot which meant I had to meet new moms, make new friends, learn new places and start a new job every time.

Detour #2 – Happily ever after? Unfortunately, that did not happen either. I found myself yet again, in a new place, divorced and with two kids. It was at that moment that I made the decision to take charge! Up to that point, I'd always let others take charge – my family, my dad and my husband! Now, it was my turn. Once again in a new, unknown territory, I decided to press forward boldly instead of packing up and moving home. That is when, unbeknownst to me, the foundation of **FABWOMEN** began.

See it is in times like these that we as women can get our brightest creations. **FAB** is my oxygen, it is what I need to get motivated. When I know that I am using this business to encourage other women that found themselves experiencing detours in their life and help them feel good about their new journey and move forward. It's funny how things work out. You think you are on the right path but for some reason, that path changes direction and you realize that it is this new path that forms you to the woman you have now become.

Website: www.fabwomen.me

Email: Shanna@fabwomen.me

Leveraging Social Media to Grow Your Business
Tangela Seals

Not long ago, all you needed were multiple degrees and a minimum of ten years of experience to qualify for a job that would allow you to earn a decent living. There was also a time when you needed decades of corporate experience before being able to launch your own business successfully. Today, none of these things are necessary for you to become a successful entrepreneur who owns a profitable business. Entrepreneurs in their twenties and teens have built businesses that earn multiple six figures - and even millions of dollars - in profit every single year. Most of these entrepreneurs do not have a ton of experience, and some haven't even been formally educated.

What set these entrepreneurs apart from the rest of the crowd? Social media is the vessel that completely changed the game for entrepreneurs.

Let me give you an example. If your sister posts on Facebook about an amazing new restaurant, you are likely to visit that restaurant at some point because you trust your sister's opinion. Since she raved about her experience at the restaurant, you know that you may also have a pleasurable experience there. This example demonstrates that social media is the next best thing to word-of-mouth promotion. Therefore, if you own a business and you are not active on social media, then you are already tardy to the party.

Most business owners and aspiring entrepreneurs already know that one of the first steps in building your business is growing your community. Your product or service is likely not one-size-fits-all.

Your business has been crafted for a specific type of person and you need to determine exactly who that person is. Once you discover who your ideal client or customer is, you can dive full speed ahead into social media because now you know exactly to whom you are marketing your business. An important thing to keep in mind is who the decision maker is. Who will decide whether your product or service will be purchased? If the investment for your business offering is a few thousand dollars, there are many people who will want to consult with their spouse before they make the purchase. Always keep in mind that you are not just marketing to your ideal customer; you are also trying to convince the decision maker.

The first step to leveraging social media to launch a profitable business is to establish which social media channels you are going to use. There are a ton of platforms out there, with more and more popping up every single day. This takes us right back to the importance of knowing who your ideal client or customer is. Once you determine who your ideal client and decision maker are, you must discover exactly where they hang out online. On which social media platforms are they active?

For most entrepreneurs, the top social media platforms are Facebook, if your target customer is a young or middle-aged adult. Hop on to Instagram or Snapchat if you're marketing to a younger crowd. YouTube is great if your target customer needs to 'get to know you' before they buy. Twitter is wonderful if you have a way with words because the platform has users of all ages. If your business offering can easily be summed up into an image and your target customer is artistic, then Pinterest would be a great social channel for you to be on. Don't waste your time putting effort into social media channels on which your ideal client or customer is not active. When starting out, select two platforms to promote your business and learn how to master those platforms. Begin by creating or sourcing content, scheduling your posts, growing your audience, and increasing your engagement. Once you get into the groove of things, then you can move on to marketing on other platforms.

Knowing what to post and what not to post is one of the biggest marketing headaches for entrepreneurs to tackle. The simple answer is, post what your followers and target audience want to see. Comedic, motivational, and inspirational posts perform best. If you have controversial opinions that you like to express on social media, you should create a separate business account. If Facebook is the platform that you are going to use to grow your community, then it is necessary to create a separate page for your business from your personal page. Facebook does not like when users promote their businesses on their personal accounts as it is seen as "spammy." Your personal page is for you to talk about your life. Since your business is a part of your life, you can talk about it as much as you want on your personal page. However, you should not encourage people to sign up for anything or spend their money on your personal page. If you promote your business on your personal page too much, your account could eventually be blocked by the Facebook administrators.

When posting on your personal Facebook page, use the same content and verbiage that you would use on your business page. There could be many people following your personal page who may also be your ideal customer. Another perk of informing your personal audience of your business ventures is that they are a warm audience who already knows, likes, and trusts you. Your personal audience may also be willing to share your posts about your business on their pages, which will further expose your business offerings to new people.

Other social platforms, like Instagram, Twitter, Pinterest, YouTube, etc., will allow you to use your profile for both personal and professional purposes. Growing a loyal and engaged social media following can be quite challenging. Having two accounts means doing double the work. A boss like you knows it is better to work smarter, not harder! The general rule of thumb on these social channels is to have one account that is devoted to growing your business.

The more active you are on social media, the quicker your following will grow. In a nutshell, this means that the more active you are, the more that people will be made aware of your business. It is important to show up online when your followers are there, so pay attention to your analytics! Most social media platforms will allow you to check your analytics, which will tell you the days and times that your followers are most active. This is major because you need to show up when your followers are present. Plan out your posts so that you do not miss peak posting times when your followers are most active so that your engagement will increase. Engagement is key to ranking highly on your social media platform's algorithm. "If you aren't sure about how to access the analytics for a social media platform, you can do a Google search or look on YouTube for more information.

A great way to increase your engagement is to become someone worth following by giving your audience valuable golden nuggets of information. But don't be that person...that annoying entrepreneur who is always pushing their business offerings on others. Being pushy will drive your audience away, so use a lead magnet to warm your audience up. A lead magnet is a valuable piece of content that you give away free to people who opt-in and subscribe to your email list. Incentivize your audience to share your lead magnets by offering an additional freebie to those that share your original lead magnet. If you are promoting a lead magnet on your social media account, "bribe" your audience to share your content on their Facebook page. For example, if your lead magnet is a video training, you can ask people who opt in to your video training to share the link on their Facebook page so that they can gain access to a free workbook that goes along with your training.

From childhood, we have been trained to do what we are told, so take advantage of that. Simply telling people to comment on your posts can increase your engagement. You can also engage your audience by using calls-to-action in your posts. For example, tell your followers to leave a comment on your post that relates to the topic of the post. Ask questions in your posts and prompt your audience to respond to your questions in the comments section. Comments carry more weight than likes with the social media apps and will boost your ranking on the algorithm even more. Another way to boost engagement and rank is to use video. Video and live streams have become increasingly popular. Social platforms love users who use video, especially live streams.

Facebook is shifting toward becoming a video platform, therefore Facebook rewards users who post videos and live streams by placing their content in front of more people. Since most people have more followers on their personal pages than on their business pages, a great technique to get more likes and follows on your Facebook business page is to live stream or post a video, then share it to your personal page. This will allow your business page to rank higher on Facebook's algorithm because the platform registers shares by followers as content that users want to see. Over time, traffic and engagement on your business page will increase.

Ultimately, the fastest way to grow your following and generate leads on Facebook and other platforms is to invest in sponsored ads. Facebook is a "pay to play" platform. If you want to get new eyes on your page and your business, running paid ads will undoubtedly get you there.

Not too long ago, the rules of success (college, profession, climb the corporate ladder, retirement) were strict and rigid. Then along came the internet and suddenly, the steps to success changed. To make money in your business, you need customers. In the digital age, growing a tribe of people who rally around your business offerings has become easier than ever. Social media has made it possible for anyone to start their own business, make money, and live life on their own terms.

Tangela Seals

Tangie is a Business & Branding Strategist with degrees in Economics and International Relations, but she is a creative at heart. She uses her skills to help small businesses by creating websites, blog posts, and revenue-generating content. Tangie is passionate about helping companies implement digital and social media marketing strategies to spread brand awareness and increase sales.

Recently she became a co-host and co-owner of a podcast syndicated out of Dallas, Texas, very aptly called The Hustle Babes. Tangie brings the millennial vision and belief in achieving business goals to all the companies whose creative department she helps develop.

Even though her experience is not vast in years, it encompasses successes in the event planning industry, as well as building an organization for professionals within the beauty industry.

Email: tangelacseals@yahoo.com

Instagram: www.instagram.com/tangieseals

Website: www.tangieseals.com

Hook Hot Leads with CONTENT
Sharvette Mitchell

Content is king. You will see this all over the Internet. You will also see this all over blogs and Google. Content is king because content is what you need to share online so that you can hook your leads and potential clients. It's just like fishing. You have to put some bait on the hook. You drop the hook in the water and that attracts the fish. You pull the fish right up and there you go...You've got a fish. That's what content is in our world of online marketing with social media and blogging. It is the hook that will grab and snag your leads and potential clients.

A question that may be on your mind is, "Okay. What's the next step? How do I get this content?" Yes, it's easy to, say, do a Facebook Live post, write a LinkedIn post, craft a blog, or share a tip, but where are you getting this content from? Well, you have three options, in my humble opinion. You can either create it, curate it, or repurpose it.

Create Content

Let me just say this... you always have content. You are not in a deficit when it comes to content. I want you to have that mindset right off the bat because you are not lacking anything when it comes to content. I believe you already have content but maybe you're not thinking about it in that way or you just haven't put the puzzle pieces together.

Your Website
Number one, if you have a website, there is content on your website. You had to come up with a Home page, About page, and

you had to come up with services or products. There's information on your website that talks about the problems you solve and the solutions you offer. That can be used as content on social media or online.

If you have a blog on your site, that content can also be used to attract leads. Use this content in your emails and on social media. Does your website have brochures that describe services or describe things of interest to your target audience? Share that in other places! The content that you're posting and creating is going to hook the leads and your ideal client because it helps them to connect with your brand.

Presentation Materials

Those of you that are speakers and coaches, I guarantee, can go back and look at presentation material you have in PowerPoint. Simply pull content out of your PowerPoint presentation to share on a Facebook Live post, in emails, or that you can share anywhere on social media. Locate your files and presentation materials because they are a gold mine. One presentation may give you a month's worth of content to share!

Pictures

I'm sure you could scroll through your mobile phone and see pictures that would be interesting and intriguing for your target audience. Share those pictures, which I like to call "behind the scenes" pictures, with your audience. If you go to events as an author, consultant, or speaker, ask someone to capture some pictures of you in action. That's great content because people feel like you brought them along for the ride. Remember, a picture is worth a thousand words...

Your Mind

I also want to submit to you that your wonderful brilliance in your brain is content. You're in business because you have information; you have an expertise or a skillset that other people need. You are an expert at whatever it is that you are promoting online and on social media. There is genius in your head that you can share to hook your hot leads.

Your Life Is Content

I heard Rachel Luna, best-selling author of the book, Successful People are Full of C.R.A.P. (Courage. Resilience. Authenticity. Perseverance), say, "Your life is content." I absolutely live by this. This is something that I say to myself. She went on to say, "Stop driving yourself crazy trying to come up with content. Your entire life is content."

I want you to pause and reflect on these quotes if you have any anxiety about how to create content. Just because you are reading this, I believe and I trust that you have much to offer the world. Think about everyday life as content. If something happens at the grocery store, if you see something on TV, if you have a great phone call with a customer, figure out how it can tie into your business. Do any of those experiences relate to a product or service you offer? Tie that in and share it. Your life is content...

Curate and Repurpose Content

Now, think about a museum curator. A museum curator comes up with exhibits. It might be an Egyptian exhibit or a historical African exhibit. A museum curator looks at their current artifacts and inventory and they pull together things that they have that relate to the exhibit. But the second thing a museum curator does is they will go to other museums and solicit artifacts, sculptures, and paintings that pertain to their exhibit. I want you to turn into a museum curator!

You can save time and energy on content creation by either curating your own content or looking at someone else's content. Yes, looking at someone else's content!

Okay, so let's first deal with curating your own content. Again, this is all about saving you time, saving you energy, and being efficient and quick about utilizing content as a marketing tool.

Go back to old social media posts...It could have even been from two years ago... and repost that content. Look through your content, curate your own content, and reshare it. Why? You have new followers who never saw your content the first time. You also have those who have been following you and connected to you but they didn't see it the first time you posted it. Keep in mind that there are people online at various times during the day. Perhaps you posted the content in the morning but 50% of your audience does not get online until after 8:00 p.m. at night. Guess what? They missed it the first time, so post it again!

Now, let's talk about curating other people's content. Listen, this is fine to do. You don't need to create everything and you don't need to come up with everything. Just like that museum curator goes to the Smithsonian or whatever other museum to borrow artifacts, you can do the same.

Here's Five Ways You Can Curate Other People's Content

Google

Google is absolutely your friend. Anything, any kind of tip, anything related to your industry, can be searched for on Google. Use Google to locate articles, pictures, or things that other people have created that you can then share on your website, blog, or social media. Now, here's the caveat. Whenever you share other people's content, give them create for it AND add your voice to it. Make sure you add some kind of personal commentary about the content.

Blogs

Blogs are amazing for content because they are written to share advice, give people guidance, and provide people with tips. You can utilize other people's blogs and their blog posts and share that content online. You don't need to actually write the blog. You don't even need to have your own blog at all. Your purpose is to share content that is attractive to your leads.

Articlesfactory.com

This site allows you to search for all kinds of articles that people freely write and share. You can put the articles on your website, blog, or you can simply find a quote that you want to share on social media. Simply give credit to the source.

Facebook.com

I think people who aren't using the "Search Facebook" feature are missing out. You can actually search Facebook almost the same way you search on Google. The powerful thing about searching Facebook is that they will show you content that already has high engagement. That takes some of the guess work out of it!

YouTube.com

Video content is great to share on your blog, in emails, and on social media. YouTube has a plethora of content for you to share and you do not have to get in front of a camera to create it.

So now do you see that content is all around you, and you just need to weave it together to tell the story of your brand? Put together a content exhibit of your brand. Think about it: in that instance, you're pulling together pieces and items and things that will relate to your brand. That content will entice those that are watching you, those that want to do business with you, and those that are ready for your service or your product. You are hooking hot leads with your content and telling the story of your brand.

Sharvette Mitchell
Coach. Web Designer. Speaker.

Sharvette is a graduate of Virginia Commonwealth University with a Bachelor of Science in Marketing. She has 25 years of experience in corporate America in the field of training & development and Consumer Compliance. Sharvette provides web design services for female entrepreneurs so that they can generate revenue with an amazing online brand. In conjunction to web design, Sharvette is a Coach & Trainer and conducts personal & group training and seminars with emphasis on the use of social networking sites, branding and online marketing tools.

Website: www.SharvetteMitchell.com

The Sharvette Mitchell Radio Show
Website: www.Sharvette.com

Phone: 804-690-5143

www.Facebook.com/Sharvette

www.Facebook.com/MitchellProductions

www.Twitter.com/Sharvette

The Missing Link in Your Sales Conversations
Shelly Pereira

In 2015, I attended a conference in Dallas where I met Cheri Tree, Founder of the B.A.N.K.™ Personality Sales Training System and best-selling author of *Why They Buy*. While listening to Cheri's presentation, I remember experiencing several "aha" moments while thinking about a couple of prospects I didn't close prior to the conference. Now I knew exactly why I didn't close at that time and how I could reach out with a different approach. Where was this powerful tool when I first started selling? In my 25-year sales career, I haven't come across a new method that makes such an impact until B.A.N.K. I realized this is the ultimate tool to teach others how to adapt their sales presentation and scripts for maximum results.

What Is B.A.N.K.?

B.A.N.K. is comprised of four personality codes, **Blueprint**, **Action**, **Nurturing**, and **Knowledge**, which influence the way we make buying decisions. Each personality has a set of values that make us unique. Think of this as your behavioral DNA. These values and behaviors make you more receptive to certain approaches, communication styles, and decision outcomes.

Most personality systems are based in psychology and focus on the individual. B.A.N.K. is "other" focused and categorizes people according to how they buy or say "yes" in the sales process. B.A.N.K. is the only methodology scientifically validated to predict buying behavior in less than 90 seconds.

The Biggest Mistake in Sales

You commonly have the wrong sales conversation with your prospect. Why? The majority of us have one rehearsed sales presentation we use over and over again. We communicate and sell based on what is important to us, so we essentially speak the wrong language to three out of four personality types. B.A.N.K. teaches you how to have sales conversations based on what is important to your buyer. Did you know people actually prefer to buy from someone just like them who shares similar values?

How Does B.A.N.K. Work?

In order to adapt your sales approach, it is important to understand your prospect's full B.A.N.K. Code as we are a combination of all four personality types.

Let's take a brief look at each of the four B.A.N.K. Codes which consist of key values, motivations, clues, likes, dislikes, and personal characteristics.

Who Is a Blueprint (B)?

Blueprint personalities are totally "inside the box," which keeps them in their comfort zone. Their key motivation is feeling safe and protected ... anything that feels risky to them will likely lose a sale. Blueprints are conservative and punctual. When working with them, be on time, prepared, and follow through with what you say you will do. Blueprints love details and are great organizers and planners. They value proven systems that deliver results.

Blueprint Core Values:

1. Stability
2. Structure
3. Systems
4. Planning
5. Processes
6. Predictability
7. Responsibility
8. Duty
9. Rules
10. Credentials
11. Titles
12. Tradition

Who Is an Action (A)?

Action personalities are the total opposite of the Blueprint. They are not afraid to take risks. They value fun, freedom, and flexibility. Their key motive is to be the best and to win. One of the values that sets Action people apart from the other personalities is they are high-performance individuals and take massive action to achieve results. They want to get to the bottom line quickly.

Action Core Values:

1. Freedom
2. Flexibility
3. Spontaneity
4. Action
5. Opportunity
6. Excitement
7. Attention
8. Stimulation
9. Competition
10. Winning
11. Fun
12. Image

Who Is a Nurturing (N)?

Nurturing personalities value relationships and meaningful connections above all else. They are some of the nicest people you will ever meet and have happy, friendly faces. In order to do business with them, be authentic, get to know them on a deeper level, build trust, and learn to speak their language. Nurturers make decisions based on intuition and with their heart. Show them you care about what is in their best interest.

Nurturing Core Values:

1. Relationships
2. Authenticity
3. Personal Growth
4. Significance
5. Teamwork
6. Involvement
7. Community
8. Charity
9. Ethics
10. Harmony
11. Morality
12. Contribution

Who Is a Knowledge (K)?

Knowledge personalities are smart, serious, logical, and innovative problem solvers. They need a lot more information than other personality types and want to know they are making the best decision at the best value. K's are motivated by being right and don't want to make a wrong decision. They love to have conversations with other experts. When selling to them, be credible, logical in your approach, and don't try to rush them to make a decision. Generally, a Knowledge personality will sell themselves after doing their research and due diligence. Look for ways you can help them move forward at their own pace in the decision process.

Knowledge Core Values:

1. Learning
2. Intelligence
3. Logic
4. Self-Mastery
5. Technology
6. Research and Development
7. Science
8. Universal Truths
9. Expertise
10. Competence
11. Accuracy
12. The Big Picture

As you can see, these four B.A.N.K. Codes are very different. So, doesn't it make sense to take a distinct sales approach with each of them?

How Do You Apply B.A.N.K.?

We teach you how to crack the code of your prospects and adapt your sales approach to each personality. It is important to sell to the first two codes and avoid their last two, which could lose the deal. In my experience meeting with prospects, I find most people go back and forth in their first two codes. Your goal is to sell to the code that is present in your meeting. A prospect may start out in their first code, then shift into their second code, or vice versa.

For example, I had a meeting with a Nurturing, Knowledge personality type. I started the meeting in a very nurturing way, using a friendly conversational approach. I spent a lot more time getting to know the prospect and building a genuine connection. I noticed she began to shift into her Knowledge code. So it was important that I made this shift along with her. A high-scoring Knowledge person likes to work with an expert in their subject matter, learn something new, and get in-depth information. So, I spent the second half of the meeting discussing her current challenges, sales best practices, strategy, and how I would approach working with her. Using the B.A.N.K. methodology resulted in an $18,000 contract in less than 30 days.

Many people with whom I talk (mostly Nurturing personalities) believe you need to spend several meetings over many months to build a long-term relationship and really get to know your prospect before doing business with them. This is simply not true. If you take the right approach, you can accomplish building the relationship in your first meeting. The key is to understand your buyer, know your sales objective, uncover their needs, and have the right sales conversation to move the deal forward.

During one of my recent B.A.N.K. trainings, a direct sales person with 20 years of experience realized she was only effective in selling to Action and Nurturing personality types. (Her own B.A.N.K. Code is Nurturing, Action.) She now knows why she is not successful selling to Blueprint and Knowledge prospects. She learned how to change her approach, sales scripts, and the products she recommends based on her client's code. Talk about what I call a "BANKable" moment! This is an invaluable skill that will result in growing her business.

I recently delivered a two-day sales training. The team realized they have been conducting all their sales presentations from their own point of view, which have been negatively impacting some of their outcomes. They are now adapting their approach to speak to the personality code of their prospect. One sales rep shared that after changing her sales conversation to two different buyers in the weeks after the training, she generated $5000 in two new sales. She had a Nurturing conversation with one prospect by appealing to her need to take care of herself in the same way she is caring for everyone else in her life. Then with an Action personality, she had a high-level discussion. By getting to the bottom line quickly, appealing to his ego, and suggesting the right options for the busy executive, his only question to her was, "do you take American Express?"

Grow Your Business

In conclusion, B.A.N.K. makes selling easier for entrepreneurs and gives seasoned salespeople a competitive edge to increase revenue and decrease sales cycles.

Shelly Pereira
President and Founder
Verance Consulting

Shelly Pereira, President and Founder of Verance Consulting, works with salespeople and entrepreneurs to solve sales challenges, improve performance and increase results.

Shelly is an award-winning salesperson selling over $35 million during her 25-year sales career in the printing industry. She has held a variety of leadership positions in sales, management and marketing. Shelly is a Certified Coach, Licensed and Certified B.A.N.K.™ Personality Sales Trainer and a Certified Hatchbuck Partner. In 2017, Shelly won the B.A.N.K. Icon Award for Blueprints. She serves on the national executive board of the Executive Women's Golf Association. Shelly graduated from Marshall University with a bachelor's degree in business.

About Verance Consulting

Verance Consulting is a sales training and consulting company teaching salespeople and business owners how to improve performance and increase sales results.

Verance Consulting Services:
- Sales Training and Development
  - B.A.N.K. Personality Training: Sales & Communication
  - Traditional Selling Skills
- Sales Consulting
  - Strategy, Sales Process Improvement, Sales Performance
  - CRM, Sales & Marketing Automation

Email: shelly@veranceconsulting.com

Website: https://www.veranceconsulting.com

LinkedIn: www.linkedin.com/in/shellypereira

Improving Client Retention Through Client Appreciation

Dianne Hentzen

Unappreciated. That was our exact perception when my husband and I recently attempted to see the latest Star Wars movie.

Our daughters had surprised us with a generous movie gift E-card. We were attempting to use the remaining balance of this E-Card. When we handed the cashier the E-Card with the remaining balance, we set off a chain of events, resulting in an embarrassing confrontation in the middle of the theater lobby with the General Manager. Unbeknownst to us, when we previously used the gift E-Card, we were not given the proper receipt which would enable us to reuse the balance of our gift.

We were treated like idiots since the theater personnel thought we should have known better. When we refused to accept their blame, they changed tactics and treated us like scam artists. After a heated 20-minute discussion, the manager magnanimously allowed us into the theater. We were seething when we finally sat down to view the movie.

As a side note, we never heard back from the theater as the manager had promised. We still have a remaining gift balance that we can't use!

Can you relate to that abandoned feeling when you are slighted and disregarded by a company you have patronized? According to the Small Business Administration, 66% of customers will leave a business because they perceive that the company does not care about them. I can attest since we will not be returning to that theater in the future. Rather than being accommodating and apologetic, the theater blamed us for their error. The manager had an ideal opportunity to create enthused fans, but instead he created infuriated ex-patrons.

The Value of Client Appreciation

Client Appreciation is an invaluable component in retaining and growing business relationships with existing clients.

Strengthening key relationships fosters:

1. Repeat business

2. Referrals

3. Customer Loyalty and Raving Fans

Repeat Business

Owners, did you realize that it costs six to seven times more to acquire a new client as it does to retain an existing one? Therefore, repeat business is important. Unfortunately, most businesses primarily focus on client acquisition rather than client retention. They choose the more expensive route – marketing to new customers – to expand their business.

As business owners, it is essential for our clients to feel special and appreciated. We aspire for them to love doing business with us time and again. Is your relationship with your customer everything it should be? How do you demonstrate you care beyond the sale?

Begin somewhere, even if you are just starting your business. Factor client appreciation into your annual business investment budget. One way to do this is to reinvest a percentage of your profit back into retention. What is your clients' loyalty worth to you: 1%, 2% - even 5%?

If you are unable to share your affection with all your customers, select the crucial ones as a starting point. Consider using the 80/20 rule – if roughly 80% of your business comes from 20% of your customers, put your efforts for customer appreciation with those clients in the 20%.

Referrals

Companies are in the customer experience business - customer service is no longer enough. How do you want your clients to feel? If they are pleased, they will happily send their family and friends to you. Existing customers and referrals are impacted by client appreciation, so focus on leveraging that revenue source.

To develop such a cohort of customers who are excited to do business with you and who want to share their positive experiences with others, there are various strategies to implement to promote customer care:

1. Make it easy to do business with your company.

2. Be responsive, take responsibility, and prove you are reliable.

3. Give more perceived value.

4. Go above and beyond.

5. Focus on the customers and brighten their day.

Customer Loyalty and Raving Fans

The economics of customer loyalty are remarkable, especially when you consider the Customer Lifetime Value (CLV). CLV is a profit prediction assigned to the entire length of the customer relationship. It is a marketing tool to determine the current value of expected income from one customer. This is useful in determining how you allocate your business resources.

Instill loyalty and create Raving Fans by going above and beyond. Let them know that they are truly valued. Who does not want a volunteer salesforce of Raving Fans? Expressing your gratitude and personalizing business relationships strengthen customer loyalty.

Another way to increase customer loyalty is through a client appreciation program. Employing a client appreciation program does not have to be a big expenditure of time or money but it will create a significant impact. It is not an expense; in fact, it is a smart business investment with long term benefits.

Three Simple Steps to Develop Customer Appreciation

My business is all about helping other people to show appreciation to their clients. Here are three tips I've learned as an expert in the field of appreciating people!

Step 1
Tell clients that you are thankful for their business. It seems logical, but I was taken aback by a recent comment I received from a client. After accepting a check from her for my services, I

thanked her. She immediately asked why *I* was thanking <u>her</u>. I explained that I believe it is common courtesy to thank clients when receiving both their business and payment. Warmly acknowledge your gratitude to your customers since they are the lifeblood of your business.

Reaching out to a previous client is another great opportunity to thank them as well as follow up on the service/product that you provided.

Step 2

Express your regard and recognize your client with a *card*: a handwritten note, E-Card, or greeting card. There are many online card platforms; I use AmericanGreetings.com for sending E-Cards and SendOutCards.com for mailing physical cards. Both are convenient methods to reach clients in a thoughtful way.

SendOutCards allows you to devise a systematic way of staying in front of your prospects and for clients to keep you at the top of their mind. When you remain top of mind, your clients will contact you instead of your competition when they need your service/product again. A yearly *relationship marketing plan* can be designed with greeting cards for various occasions: expressing gratitude, sending holiday or birthday wishes, congratulating anniversaries, and even promoting business. The SendOutCards concept is easy, customized, and affordably priced. There is also the added convenience of including gifts.

Have you ever been surprised by a thank you card from your contractor? Was that "thank you" accompanied by brownies or another treat? My electrician sets himself apart by using SendOutCards to express his "chocolatey" thanks to his customers. Do you think they will use his services again and refer him to others? You bet they will!

Step 3

Really make an impression by giving an *unexpected gift*. Your very best clients deserve it and your *referral partners* do, too. "Surprise and Delight" is a great strategy!

Anytime is an appropriate time to give a gift. Look for reasons to celebrate your clients! There are so many reasons to let your clients know how important they are to you, especially during a lengthy convalescence or illness.

If you have the option, do not allow your appreciation efforts to be lost amidst a holiday frenzy. Instead, choose another time other than the holiday season to stand out. Make it fun and memorable.

There are many gifting options, but here are some to stir up your creativity:

1. *Personalized* gifts and gift baskets.

2. Free upgrade to your service or product.

3. The gift of your time.

4. Spotlight them on Social Media.

5. Donation to a *client's* favorite charity.

6. Experiences: Tickets to sporting events, a museum membership, complimentary local tours, etc.

7. Client Celebration party.

Successful gifting begins with intelligence-gathering. Take time to note your client's likes, dislikes, and passions. There is huge merit in taking the time to get to know your clients. Case in point: my client shared her client's interests. Knowing this information allowed me to select a locally-sourced vintage atlas page, framed in reclaimed wood. That client was thrilled to have the piece and said it was her absolute favorite gift ever!

One of my other clients knew her client's favorite movie series, so we created and delivered a funky Star Wars-themed gift container. He knew the "force" was with him!
Locally-sourced items are often client favorites. Consider your strategic partners' services and products; those might be the perfect choice. Support one another as you grow your businesses.

Consumable gifts can be a challenge, especially if you do not personally know the recipient. Many people possess food intolerances or allergies. However, some company policies dictate only consumables can be given. If you must follow these guidelines, I recommend providing an assortment of food items, including some that are allergen-free.

Map out a client appreciation strategy on your calendar. As you implement your plan, following up with clients and prospects is key. It opens dialogue and engagement. Be consistent. Sometimes your results look like the tip of the iceberg, but your impact reaches far below the surface. Serve your clients well and they will stay with you.

Stand Out from Your Competition

Client appreciation is not meant to be rocket science. Rather, it is a simple principle which is easily overlooked, especially by businesses that are overwhelmed with daily responsibilities.

The quality of your business/client relationship may be the only aspect that sets you apart in your industry. How are your customers perceiving your business? Make sure to *intentionally* strengthen your business relationships and maximize your referral potential. Bear in mind the importance of Customer Lifetime Value. The goal is to retain your clients and give your salesforce of Raving Fans something to talk about!

I am closing this chapter with my favorite quote from Peter Shankman, the author of *Zombie Loyalists*. It is a great sentence that sums up the importance of customer service, appreciation, and loyalty:

"You get the customers you _want_ by being beyond awesome to the customers you _have_".

Dianne Hentzen
Founder and CEO
Caring Touch Concierge

As the founder of Caring Touch Concierge, Dianne enjoys translating thoughtfulness into B2B client appreciation. She adds the personal touches that set her clients apart. Dianne provides fun and memorable expressions of gratitude to strengthen long term business relationships.

During her time as a stay-at-home mom, Dianne employed her DIY skills serving her church and community by leading women's activities and children's craft programs. Sharing hospitality and caring for the needs of others ultimately led to the creation of her business. One aspect of the business includes acting as a companion to Seniors by assisting around their homes, running errands and reducing their isolation. The underlying premise is to let Seniors know they matter and are appreciated. Another facet of her business involves employing the same principle of gratitude, but in the business world. She supports companies in their efforts to retain their customers through her client appreciation program: "Say It, Ink It, Gift It."

When Dianne is not developing client appreciation strategies for local businesses and entrepreneurs, she is spending time with family, gardening, serving on the leadership team of FABWOMEN, or volunteering at church.

Email: dianne@caringtouchconcierge.com

Website: www.caringtouchconcierge.com

Three Common Business Tax Myths to Dismiss
Shan-Nel D. Simmons

With the help of technology, we have access to more information now than we will ever need in our lifetimes. Unfortunately, there is an overabundance of misinformation shared online between friends, family, and even from other professionals about everything. The wrong information can result in very costly consequences for you, especially when it comes to taxes. To save you from a surprise tax bill in the future, I am going to clarify three common business tax myths you should dismiss right now:

Myth #1: "My business, or side hustle, did not make much money this year, so I do not have to report anything."

There is an odd misconception floating around that if a business or side hustle makes little to no money during the year that the business/side hustle is not a "real business." Since it is believed to not be a "real business," the taxpayer believes nothing should be reported about the business/side hustle on their income tax return. This kind of thinking is simply not true.

First, you must understand that all income is taxable unless the tax code states otherwise.1 Therefore, if the income you receive is from a taxable source, such as money earned for your services, or commission paid to you for products you sold, then that income is also reportable on an income tax return.2 Even if the

---

1 IRC §61(a)
2 IRC §6012, Regulation §1.6012-1(a)

net profit (or net loss) from your business/side hustle combined with your other sources of income, your filing status, and your age result in you not being required to file an income tax return, you may still want to file a return if you want to get back any withholdings you paid during to year or to receive any possible refundable tax credits. If the business/side hustle was set up to be taxed as a C Corporation, you are always required to file a return every year.[3]

Another reason you will want to file your business returns every year is because a tax return is a common document requested by banks and other institutions. Tax returns help these institutions to verify your income, review profit and loss patterns, and look for other qualifications to approve your business for loans, certifications, grants, etc. Not having a tax return with your business activity reported could mean missed opportunities for you and your business.

Myth #2: "To save money, I will treat all of my workers as 1099 contractors."

Paying your employees' wages is usually one of the costliest operating expenses for a business owner. Add employment taxes, unemployment taxes, health benefits, worker's compensation, and other employee benefits to those wages, and it is easy to see why a business owner will consider changing all their workers from employees to independent contractors to increase profits and to improve their cash flow.

But even though employees are pricey, you cannot switch employees to contractors as a quick fix to save some dollars

---

[3] Regulation §1.6012-2(a)

unless the facts support such a change. Therefore, as a business owner, you must consider these three categories per the IRS[4] to determine if a worker should be treated as an independent contractor or as an employee:

1. Behavioral control

2. Financial control

3. Relationship

Behavioral Control

Behavioral control exists for an employee when "the business has the right to direct and control the work performed by the worker, even if that right is not exercised." Some examples of employee behavioral control are conducting annual performance reviews; providing training, whether it is one time or ongoing; providing tools and supplies for employees to complete the work; and requiring a uniform. These kinds of behavioral controls will either not exist or will be less restrictive for an independent contractor.

Financial Control

Financial control is more than controlling how much your worker is paid. An independent contractor is usually free to secure other jobs within the same industry from other businesses, whereas an employee will encounter a conflict of interest for doing the same.

---

[4] Internal Revenue Service, Understanding Employee vs. Contractor Designation (2017), Tax Fact Sheets (FS-2017-09, July 20, 2017), Retrieved from https://www.irs.gov/newsroom/understanding-employee-vs-contractor-designation

An independent contractor usually cannot get job-related expenses reimbursed (unless it is included in their invoice.) But an employee usually can get a reimbursement once an expense report is submitted with supporting receipts attached.

Relationship

Lastly, what is the relationship between the business and the worker? Employees are expected to complete tasks for the normal operations of a business indefinitely (or until they resign or are fired.) An independent contractor usually works under a contract which outlines when the job will start and when the job will end.

Is the worker eligible to receive benefits? Independent contractors are not provided benefits such as health insurance. These are a few examples of the facts you must consider when trying to classify your workers.

If a business owner classifies a worker as an independent contractor erroneously, the business will be liable for employment tax for each worker classified incorrectly. Also, providing a 1099-MISC does not automatically make a worker an independent contractor.

If you have provided workers a 1099-MISC when you should have treated them as a W-2 employee, there are relief and voluntary disclosure programs available to fix your mistake and to help you avoid penalties.

Myth #3: "Since I know I will receive a refund, I can take as long as I like to file a return to get my money back."

If you are certain you should receive a refund for any tax year you need to file, you need to file the return within two years from when the money was paid – not two years after the return was due.5 It is important to make this distinction because the money refunded on a return filed in April was actually paid in the prior year before the return's due date. So, by the typical due date in April, if you have not filed a return to claim your refund, you will roughly have only 20 more months to file a return to get your money back. This can be particularly interesting for you as a business owner who make estimated tax payments because first quarter payments are paid an entire year prior to due date before a return is due.

For example, let's say Taxpayer A's 2016 income tax return was due to be filed in April 2017. Because of other transactions during the 2016 tax year, Taxpayer A knew she would get back all her estimated tax payments in a refund. Taxpayer A paid estimated tax payments in April 2016, in July 2016, in October 2016, and in January 2017 but chose not to file her 2016 income tax return until September 2018. Taxpayer A will not get back the estimated payments she paid in April 2016 and in July 2016 because by September 2018 it is has been more than two years since she paid them.

Therefore, it is important to file timely regardless of if you owe taxes or if you will receive a refund. Not filing a return timely can cost you either way. The goal is to always pay only what you

---

5 IRC §6511(a)

legally have to pay in taxes, and then keep the rest either in your business, or even better, in your pockets and purses.

Knowing the truth about these common tax myths will save you more than just money and time as a business owner. Being knowledgeable about your taxes will also keep you and your business in good standing with the IRS and your respective state tax authority; and that kind of peace of mind while running your business is priceless.

Shan-Nel D. Simmons, EA MBA
Tax Pro & Founder
Nel's Tax Help, LLC

Shan-Nel D. Simmons, EA MBA is an enrolled agent with over 15 years in accounting and tax experience. She is a former IRS revenue agent who performed tax audits for individuals and small businesses. She currently owns and operates Nel's Tax Help, LLC providing tax and accounting services to individuals and businesses. She also wrote A.S.K.ing for Success: My Faith Walk from Employee to Entrepreneur, available now on Amazon.

Phone: 443.868.7629

Fax: 443.868.7652

Book appointments at https://nelstaxhelp.as.me

Website: https://www.nelstaxhelp.com

Finding Financial Serenity

Sorana Blackfoot

I started my financial education in the U.S. with Suze Orman and Robert Kiyosaki, and I always strived to achieve the financial freedom they taught me about. And through my journey toward financial freedom, I heard Tony Robbins explain about "the science of achievement" and "the art of fulfilment". And this cemented my commitment to achieve financial serenity.

Financial serenity is a combination of financial freedom and the serenity brought on by feelings of accomplishment and fulfilment. This is the result of achieving worthy goals and reaching significance by being able to give freely to something one is passionate about (whether that is time or money). I learned from Zig Ziglar that financial independence means you can do what you want when you want. My goal then became taking women – and a few good men – to the next level, and guiding them to financial serenity: a step beyond freedom and independence.

According to statistics, getting out of debt or saving more money – or even achieving financial freedom – is a popular New Year's resolution, second only to losing weight. The problem with setting this as an annual goal – over and over again – is that it really is wishful thinking, and not a well thought out plan. Therefore, the resolution is renewed the following year, rarely with any significant success. Most people want to make a leap from the "have-not" to the "have" column when it comes to their finances. They feel that they can triple their income, or annihilate their debt, within the year. Tony Robbins wisely said that "most people overestimate what they can do in a year and underestimate what they can do in a decade."

Instead of expecting results in a year, the most likely approach to achieve a financial goal is the "slight edge" – per Jeff Olson, in his book with the same title. He talks about doing small things every day that will compound over time to achieve big results. While this approach can work with any goals, from health and fitness, to relationships and personal improvement, I believe it is the only way to achieve lasting financial goals.

For owners who want to grow their business to the point where it becomes their retirement vehicle, reinvesting all their earnings back into the business might seem like the smart thing to do. However, this approach may prove a disastrous financial sacrifice in the long run. According to the sensible principle of diversification, you should never put all your eggs in one basket – and when that basket is your own business, especially if it is a service-based business that relies heavily on you, that may be a very dangerous path to follow.

A wiser decision may be to save some of the money earned through the business in a retirement   account – either pre-tax or after-tax – that will accumulate over time. This type of account will be there when the business owner is ready to retire. Besides the tax advantages of this plan, the main benefit consists in the fact that the retirement money is not directly tied into the business, and it is protected from any hardships that the business may encounter. In addition, the account will be available when the owner of the business wants or has to retire.

Most people are familiar with the term "compound interest" but that is usually in an abstract sense. Often people are familiar with the fact that compound interest is important, and that it can work in their favor or against them. And for the majority of people, that is where their knowledge gets blurry. They do not understand that the more time they have, the more they can benefit from the effects of the compound interest. Some of the most frequently used examples show friends who started saving for retirement at different times. While one starts in their 20's and only saves for about 10 years, the other starts saving at the same time the first one stops and continues saving until retirement age. Due to compound interest, the first friend ends up with more money at the time of retirement. Depending on the amounts invested and the interest percentage decided, the difference between the friends' savings can range from tens of thousands to some hundreds of thousands of dollars.

The difference between the two friends comes not from the amount saved but from the time they used to invest. The more time you give the compound interest to work for you, the more your savings grow, while the interest gains interest upon interest.

I'm not going to get on my soap box lamenting the lack of financial education from the U.S. school system. I will state that it is important to raise the level of understanding for all the people growing up in an economy which is so very different from the one experienced by their parents and grandparents. While the good news is that more and more people start businesses and/or become self-employed, the bad news is that these people's financial security (safe present and future) is in their own hands, since their employers are no longer present to provide the benefits that will take care of them in the long run.

Another reason that most solopreneurs make the decision to put all of their income back into the business is that they think that it will all pay off in the future because they will make more money and, in the end, can sell the business. Unfortunately, most of the time, this is not a solid exit strategy. Nobody wants to buy your job. Therefore, the only way to have a sellable business is by building systems within your business that can be followed and duplicated.

For someone who has a job, the retirement planning is often set in place by the employer, and all they have to do is follow their employer's system. Even with all the steps already planned, a large number of Americans do not take advantage of the offers. And the scary part is that among solopreneurs and the self-employed (without the path already designed for them), the numbers are even higher.

There are some scary statistics I want to share: only two out of three Americans save for retirement currently (according to a statistic from 2017). And if this is not bad enough, more than half of the ones who save have less than $10,000 in their retirement account. Yet surveys say that 51% of Americans feel they are saving enough. A recent article stated: "Transamerica found that only about half of workers feel they are building a nest egg that will sustain them in retirement" (The Motley Fool, April, 16th, 2017). While the article implies there are not enough people who are comfortable with their level of savings, my first reaction is: how can that many people even feel they have enough? Reading the statistics, I realized that only about 30% of the U.S. population has more than $10,000 in retirement savings. And with that being the case, where does the extra 21% of people get their feelings from? Did I scare you yet?

As entrepreneurs, solopreneurs and self-employed increase in numbers all across America, this is a unique opportunity for them to change these statistics. I'm not saying it is easy but it is simple: there is no other way to be and feel secure in retirement than to set aside enough money to save. Often employees see their retirement savings which are coming from their employers diminish, and they have to set aside money, also. Entrepreneurs don't even have that luxury. There is no cushion that can provide a feeling of security. For those who can sell their business, there may be a stress-free retirement in sight. But the majority of small businesses – the solopreneurs and the home-based businesses – will probably never have that option.

If you own a sellable business and decide to sell it, the first thing you need to find out is its value. And you need to understand that the value you think it is worth and the amount of money that someone is willing to pay, may be two different things – as is most often the case. After having a valuation done by a third party, such as a CPA, the next best step is talking to a financial specialist who can educate you (the seller) about a few options – financial and insurance products – that can be set up by the buyer in order to increase the amount received by the seller through this transaction. This is a way to increase either the retirement income or the family protection, or both.

When selling your business is not an option – or if you want to have more money in retirement to ensure enough income – the best idea is to start saving as early as possible. Retirement savings must be a priority. And if the 10% that financial advisors advocate sounds like too huge and intimidating of a number, it is OK to start with a lower percentage. The main goal is to start. You can always increase the amount. Plus, something saved is always better than nothing saved.

And if I have convinced you to start setting money aside, you may now start worrying where that money is going to stay. The main objective is for the money you set aside to come back to you with "friends" (more money) – the more, the better. And in order for that to happen, you cannot leave it parked in a savings account. I have nothing against banks. Banks are just not a great vehicle for increasing your net worth through savings; not with an interest rate pretty close to 0%. The right type of investment and the company, as well as the status (qualified funds versus non-qualified funds), will depend on your needs, risk tolerance and when you need to have access to the money. All investments should be personalized for you. Therefore, either you are an expert, become an expert, or hire an expert to help you.

The one sure way to figure out which investment will bring you the most money is using the Rule of 72. This will show you how many years it will take for your investment to double. To find this out, you would take the interest rate you receive and divide it into 72. This number signifies the number of years it would take you before your money doubles without your adding anything extra. For a 1% interest it takes 72 years to double the money you deposit – let's not even look at under 1% (which is what you get from your regular savings account at the bank). For an 8% interest rate – the average growth of the market – it would take your money 9 years to double. Would you rather wait almost a lifetime, or would you like to double it in 9 years?

Now that you understand why it is important to have a plan to exit your business into retirement, you are ready to set a system in place. And the best thing to do is to make saving for retirement a priority. If you ever heard any financial experts talk about saving money, you are probably familiar with the phrase "pay yourself first". There is no better recipe for retirement. Whether you can direct 10% of your income towards retirement, or you need to start with a smaller amount, it is always best to start. As you get into the habit of saving, you will find it easier and more rewarding. If you struggle in the beginning and are afraid you might run out of money for current expenses, don't worry: you are not alone.

You will find creative ways to take care of current needs as soon as you have the system in place to redirect the money from current expenses to future serenity. Since not everyone has the discipline to set money aside for retirement on a regular basis, the best thing to do is to automate it – a set date, maybe a set amount. You can always change and adjust, you only need a starting point. And remember, you can always count on help from a financial professional if you lack the knowledge, the will, or the discipline to follow through.

One of my favorite quotes is a Chinese proverb: "The best time to plant a tree was 20 years ago. The next best time is now." Saving – for retirement, for a big-ticket item, or for a rainy day – works the same way. The younger you are or the earlier you start saving, the more time you have for it to grow. But it is never too late to start, and you are always better off starting to save NOW than never, or even later.

Sorana Blackfoot
Prosperity Mentor
Un-Broke Women

Sorana Blackfoot is a Prosperity Mentor, teaching women to create, preserve and transfer wealth. Through her company, Un-Broke Women, she advises women on building better relationships with their money.

Originally from Romania, Sorana has been living in Richmond since 2002. Coming to a new country, she built a successful career to make it worth the sacrifice of uprooting herself.

During her 10+ years career in finances, she learned that a lot of women are uncomfortable with their finances and therefore, are left in a very precarious situation if/when they are alone due to divorce or widowhood.

Sorana has coauthored 2 books in the last 18 months: "Remarkable Results" and "Goal for it!" and has just published her own book soon - "New World, New Dreams" – where she shares her money story.

Sorana believes in empowering women to achieve financial serenity. To this end, she organizes an annual business conference for women in Richmond Virginia in March. The goal of the conference is to empower women to design an inspiring business. By applying the knowledge shared by the expert speakers, the participants can build their business to the size of their dreams and impact their community.

Email: sorana@unbrokewomen.com

Website: http://www.unbrokewomen.com

Maximize Your ROI (Return on Ideas): Integrate New Ideas into Your Current, Crazy, Crammed Life

Sylvia Henderson

Conferences. Conventions. Expos. Trade shows. Meetings. Special events.

You have so many options available to you for professional, business, and personal development. How do you ensure that you make – and get – the most from the events you attend?

You invest time, money, and energy to attend meetings and events. You spend your days getting information, learning, connecting with people, and getting new ideas. You're excited about possibilities and your head is full of thoughts about what you want, should, or need to do when you get back home and get back to business or work. You declare your intentions and speak your commitments out loud as the event comes to an end.

Then, as you return home after the event and examine your schedule, you see the commitments you already have on your calendar and you wonder...

? What will you do next to transform your ideas to action?
? How will you squeeze in additional plans to implement your new ideas?
? Was it really "worth it" to attend that event if you fail to do something with what you got from the experience?

Before you return to your "real world" of commitments and demands, interruptions, and bright shiny objects, let's look at how you can assess all you experienced, get focused, and integrate your new ideas into your life to maximize your ROI (Return-on-Ideas). I assure you that, with intentional integration and action, you can get it done.

I'll cover this idea integration process in three parts: before, during, and after the event.

Before the Event

From the time you first learn of an event you want to attend – be it a 90-minute networking event, a full-day professional development forum, a weekend expo, or a multi-day conference or retreat – you can take certain steps to gain your maximum Return-on-Ideas. These steps apply to most types of events. Their intensity and the time you spend taking action with them will vary.

Let's start from, "There's an event I want to attend."

The first approach I recommend is to be your own reporter. Ask yourself the journalists' W5+H questions: who, what, when, where, why, and how…not necessarily in that order.

Why? Why do you want to attend?

? Do you *need* to attend?

? Are you considering attending to further develop yourself for your own business, for your career, for your organization, or for life strategies?

? Do you have alternatives available that might serve you as well, or better?

? Examine *why* you want to attend the event to make sure it will serve you.

When? Does the event fall within a time frame that you have open on your calendar?

? Can you re-arrange existing commitments – and should you – in order to attend?

? Will your business continue while you're gone?

? Does your family have a say as to the timing and prior commitments?

Where? Is the event located where you can travel to it within your budget?

? Will someone else (an employer; an organization; a sponsor) cover your travel costs?

? Are there travel advisories for the location of the event?

? Can you do other things before or after – visit people; schedule additional business; tour the area – while you are there?

? What are your transportation options?

Who?	Who will be there?
	❓ Attendees – is there an attendee listing you can review?
	❓ Speakers, facilitators, presenters, panelists – who are the influencers you want or need to meet?
	❓ For whom is the event intended? Who is the primary audience (demographic or profession)?
	❓ Who might you be able to invite to join you at the event?

What?	What is the focus of the event?
	❓ Theme? Topics? Tracks?
	❓ Agenda? Schedule?
	❓ Activities for connection?
	❓ Food – do you have special dietary needs about which you must notify the event planner?
	❓ Time outside of formal sessions?
	❓ Costs?
	❓ What issues do you want help with that attending and connecting with the "right people" will solve?
	❓ What information, stories, and experiences do *you* have that you can share with others to enrich their event experience?

How?	How will you realize your Return-on-Ideas?
	❓ How will you pay to attend?
	❓ How will you capture your ideas?
	❓ How will you communicate and implement what you learn?

I created a planning worksheet to help my clients objectively determine whether to attend an event or not in terms of its ultimate ROI.

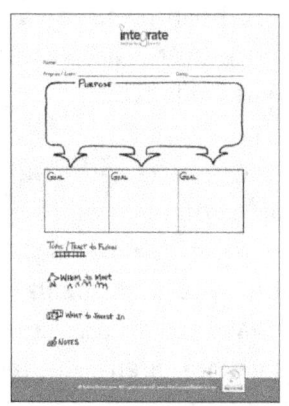

Download this planning sheet as a gift from me at bit.ly/event-roi-worksheets01.

Where do you find the event information that enables you to answer your journalist's questions? Typically you can find most of the information at the event website and in its marketing materials.

One other item to work on in preparation for your event – your budget. Take into consideration your expenses for attending to be sure you can afford to do so. Remember that attending an event is an investment not only of money, but also of your time and energy. All have value to you.

During the Event

The day arrives that you travel to and attend the event!

Review your preparations so they are top of mind. Make sure you bring something with which you can take notes – written notes! I know, you love your electronic device. Yet when you write, especially to keep track of key points, you engage multiple senses and are more-likely to retain the information you receive.

In addition to recording informational notes, also record your feelings and perceptions. When you are aware of how you feel about the information and stories you hear and people you meet, you are better able to put the tsunami of input from the event into perspective.

At the event, carry out your preparation plans. Seek out the people you planned to meet. Introduce yourself to people you sit next to in seminar sessions. Ask questions of the people with whom you eat meals. Join impromptu conversations in the hallways or at the coffee station. Participate, engage, share, absorb. Be open to different perspectives. Introduce yourself to speakers and presenters. Stop at the vendor tables in the expo section if there is one. The whole point of an in-person event is to connect and communicate, so do it.

At the end of every day of the event, or at the end of an hours-long event, this next action is key to maximizing your return-on-ideas.

After the Event

At the end of your event, make time before you return home (if you traveled long-distance), or stop at a coffee shop for a few minutes' down time before you return to work or family. Pull out your end-of-day notes.

I cannot emphasize enough how important it is to take this time to do this to maximize your Return-on-Ideas! Schedule your return time to allow for this next step.

Spread-out your end-of-day worksheets. Read through your (up to) three ideas/per day. Given a two-day event, you might have up to six ideas you want to implement. More days, more ideas.

Read through them all and identify up to five ideas you can focus on within the next 90 days. That's right…only up to five ideas. Don't worry about the rest. You won't lose them. You've written everything down from the event, and you have your summary worksheets.

Now take a blank sheet of paper and re-write those five ideas. Yes, I know you already wrote them down; yet, trust me. Re-write them now.

When you re-write them, you will word them differently. You think of them differently, especially the earlier ideas, because you've gained the perspective of the later time. You might even find that some of the other ideas are really just actions or subsets of your five focus ideas.

Once you've re-written the ideas you'll focus on, identify the actions you will take to implement those ideas from the time you arrive home or back at work, until three months from then. Focus especially on your next 30 days. Move into fast action as soon as you return so as not to lose the momentum you've gained from the energy of your event.

Identify the feelings you have about these ideas – about implementing them (fear? excitement? renewal?); about setting others to the side for now; about integrating the actions you've identified into the rest of your life as you look at your calendar; about how others will view your new ideas – all of this and more. You have to process-out your feelings as much as you have to process-out your ideas in order to do something about them.

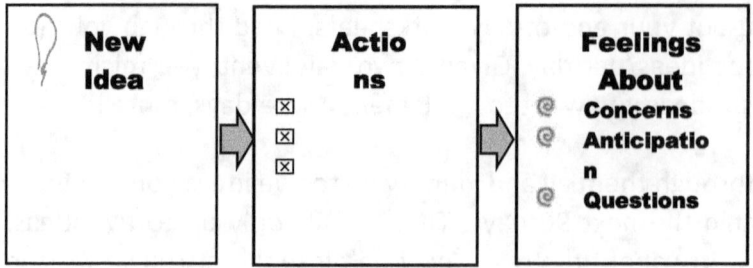

You now have an idea action chart.

If there's room below your idea chart, identify the top five people you've met with whom you most want to follow-up right away. Either tape their business cards to your chart or identify them so you can find the cards you may have scanned for their contact info. Jot a few words next to their names to identify why you want to follow-up with them and what you will ask of or give them. Be specific so that no one wastes time with, "Let's connect and get to know each other".

Integrate

Let's face it...you're not returning home to an empty calendar. You already have a full plate waiting for you, so how are you going to integrate the actions you've identified for your new ideas?

Here's where having written goals, determining what's important to you, analyzing what you can give up or say "no" to short-term, creating and sticking to a plan, and getting help with accountability all comes together. It takes work. I won't sugar-coat this. Yet the effort you put into following up on connections you make at your event and integrating the actions you identify for your ideas will bring you the ROI you seek professionally and personally.

To guide you here to integrate your ideas for maximum ROI I'll share with you the following steps. Doing them and being consistent about it is beyond the scope of this chapter. It's up to you as to how seriously you want to create the business and life you want by implementing your ideas.

So here's the integration part.

☐ Look at your goals for your business, life, year...however you've identified and written them down.
☐ Look at your vision board if you have one.
☐ Look at your calendar for the next 90 days. Identify all activities and commitments that have <u>minimal</u> impact towards your goals and vision. Take a red marker and draw a line through those activities.
  ○ Determine which of those activities you must keep on your calendar due to relationship commitments with clients, family, friends, and colleagues.
  ○ Determine which ones, and how you will, cancel or re-schedule other commitments to later times.
  ○ *Identifying them* is important to start with.
☐ Determine where you can begin to replace the minimal-impact commitments with actions towards your new ideas.
  ○ At each decision point, determine whether the new idea is more important to implement than the activity you will delete or re-schedule.
☐ Put the new actions into your schedule.
  Write them in. They are solid commitments that may include time for research, speaking with people you need to speak with, and planning your next moves.

☐ Highlight those actions and commitments with a yellow highlighter.

Now you can see what you've integrated into your life and how you've made time in your existing life to allow for the new.

The rest – the really hard stuff – is in sticking to your plan, saying "no" when you need to, grabbing opportunities you weren't even aware of with your new ideas, and checking-in with yourself or with an accountability partner every 1-to-2 weeks to mark your progress. Over time, as you keep "repeating and rinsing" this process, you will absolutely realize a Return-on-Ideas from every event you attend.

I look forward to helping you maximize your Return-on-Ideas by integrating them into your current, crazy, crammed life!

I want you to grow your business, advance your career, build strong relationships and achieve your life dreams after you have invested your time, money, and energy into the events you attend. I can help you achieve the growth and transformation you desire.

Sylvia Henderson
CEO of Springboard Training LLC
Founder of the Idea Success Network

Sylvia Henderson, Founder & CEO of Springboard Training based in the Washington DC area, brings over 30 years of corporate, association, & entrepreneur experience implementing ideas and moving employees & clients to realize results with theirs. She wrote the book on getting ideas out of your head & into action ("Hey, That's MY Idea!") available at http://bit.ly/book_HTMI_retail. Sylvia consults, speaks, hosts a cable TV show, & establishes Idea MindTeam masterminds for entrepreneurs & business leaders throughout the country.

Phone: 301.260.1538

Website: www.sylviahenderson.com

Bibliography

Why Leaders Need Emotional Intelligence:

Salovey P., and J.D. Mayer. 1990. *Emotional Intelligence. Imagination, Cognition and Personality.* 9.3: 185-211.

Bradberry, Travis, and Greaves, Jean. *Emotional Intelligence 2.0.* San Diego, California: TalentSmart; Enhanced, New edition (June 13, 2009)

The Missing Link in Your Sales Conversations

Tree, Cheri. *Why They Buy: Cracking the Personality Code to Achieve Record Sales and Real Wealth.* Aviva Publishing New York; 1 edition (July 22, 2017).

Three Common Business Tax Myths to Dismiss

IRS Code §61(a)
IRS Code §6012, Regulation §1.6012-1(a)
Regulation §1.6012-2(a)
IRC §6511(a)

Finding Financial Serenity

Tony Robbins: I Am Not Your Guru, directed by Joe Berlinger, aired July 15, 2016, on Netflix, https://www.tonyrobbins.com/documentary/.

Olson, Jeff. *The Slight Edge: Secret to a Successful Life.* Success Books (February 4, 2005).

Baukman, Marie. "10 Retirement Stats That Will Blow You Away," *The Motley Fool,* April, 16th, 2017, https://www.fool.com/retirement/2017/04/16/10-retirement-stats-that-will-blow-you-away.aspx.

Leaders Are Readers

Our authors recommend these titles:

Diana Parra:

- *Emotional Intelligence 2.0* - Travis Bradberry and Jean Greaves
- *The E-Myth Revisited: Why Most Small Businesses Don't Work and What to Do About It* - Michael E. Gerber
- *Deep Work: Rules for Focused Success in a Distracted World* - Cal Newport
- *Think and Grow Rich* - Napoleon Hill
- *Building A StoryBrand: Clarify Your Message So Customers Will Listen* - Donald Miller

Sharvette Mitchell:

- *Boss Women Pray: 31 Prayer to Increase Your Success & Spirit: The Comprehensive Prayer Guide for Entrepreneurs & Women in Business* - Kachelle Kelly
- *Are You Ready for the Yes?: How to Prep Your Personal Brand for Lucrative Opportunities* - Audria Richmond
- *Market Like a R.O.C.K. STAR: ROCK Solid Marketing Strategies to Grow Your Business Quickly*- Darnyelle A. Jervey

Shelly Pereira:

- *Why They Buy* - Cheri Tree
- *Fanatical Prospecting: The Ultimate Guide to Opening Sales Conversations and Filling the Pipeline by Leveraging Social Selling, Telephone, Email, Text, and Cold Calling* - Jeb Blount
- *Decide One Thing: The One Thing EVERY Executive Team Must Decide* - Dave Ramos

Dianne Hentzen:

- *Think and Grow Rich* - Napoleon Hill
- *Outwitting the Devil: The Secret to Freedom and Success* - Napoleon Hill
- *Beyond Positive Thinking*: Success and Motivation in the Scriptures - Jim Collins

Sorana Blackfoot:

- *Rich Dad, Poor Dad: What The Rich Teach Their Kids About Money – That The Poor And Middle Class Do Not!* - Robert Kiyosaki
- *The 9 Steps To Financial Freedom: Practical and Spiritual Steps So You Can Stop Worrying* - Suze Orman
- *The Miracle Morning for Entrepreneurs: Elevate Your SELF to Elevate Your BUSINESS* - Hal Elrod and Cameron Herold
- *The Slight Edge: Turning Simple Disciplines into Massive Success and Happiness* - Jeff Olson and John David Mann

Sylvia Henderson:

- *Think and Grow Rich* - Napoleon Hill
- *Speak and Grow Rich* - Dottie and Lilly Walters
- *The Tao of Pooh* - Ben Hoff

Stinson Mundy:

- *The E-Myth Revisited* – Michael Gerber
- *Lean Startup* – Eric Reis